Height

BLACKBIRCH PRESS
An imprint of Thomson Gale, a part of The Thomson Corporation

Detroit • New York • San Francisco • San Diego • New Haven, Conn. • Waterville, Maine • London • Munich

THOMSON

GALE

Consultant: Kimi Hosoume
Associate Director of GEMS (Great
    Explorations in Math and Science),
Director of PEACHES (Primary
    Explorations for Adults, Children,
    and Educators in Science),
Lawrence Hall of Science,
University of California,
Berkeley, California

For The Brown Reference Group plc
Text: Chris Woodford
Project Editor: Lesley Campbell-Wright
Designer: Lynne Ross
Picture Researcher: Susy Forbes
Illustrator: Darren Awuah
Managing Editor: Bridget Giles
Children's Publisher: Anne O'Daly
Production Director: Alastair Gourlay
Editorial Director: Lindsey Lowe

PHOTOGRAPHIC CREDITS
Ardea: Johan de Meester 26l; **The Brown Reference Group plc:** Edward Allwright 1,
12–13, 28, 29; **Corbis:** Bettmann 26r, Renee Lynn 13, Roy Morsch 7, Jeffrey L. Rotman 14,
Tom Stewart 20, Joseph Sohm/ChromoSohm Inc. 8; **Hemera:** 10–11t&b, 23t; **NOAA:** 15t;
Photos.com: 3–5, 9cl&bl, 9r, 15b, 17tl&tr, 22, 23b, 27; **Rex Features:** Stephen Meddle
17b, Phanie/Alix 6.

Front cover: **The Brown Reference Group plc:** Edward Allwright

LIBRARY OF CONGRESS CATALOGING-IN-PUBLICATION DATA

Woodford, Chris.
  Height / by Chris Woodford.
      p. cm. — (How do we measure?)
  Includes bibliographical references and index.
  ISBN 1-4103-0368-3 (hardcover : alk. paper) — ISBN 1-4103-0524-4 (pbk. : alk.
paper)
  1. Mensuration—Juvenile literature. 2. Altitudes—Measurement—Juvenile
literature. I. Title II. Series: Woodford, Chris. How do we measure?

  QA465.W655 2005
  516'.15—dc22

                                                                          2004022395

Printed and bound in Thailand
10 9 8 7 6 5 4 3 2 1

Contents

What is height?   4

Rulers and tape measures   6

Units of height   8

Metric heights   10

Estimating height   12

Height and depth   14

Angles and height   16

Angles and degrees   18

Height can tell you where you are   20

Climbing high   22

Habitat heights   24

Amazing heights   26

HANDS ON:

  Estimating and measuring heights   28

Glossary   30

Find out more   31

Index   32

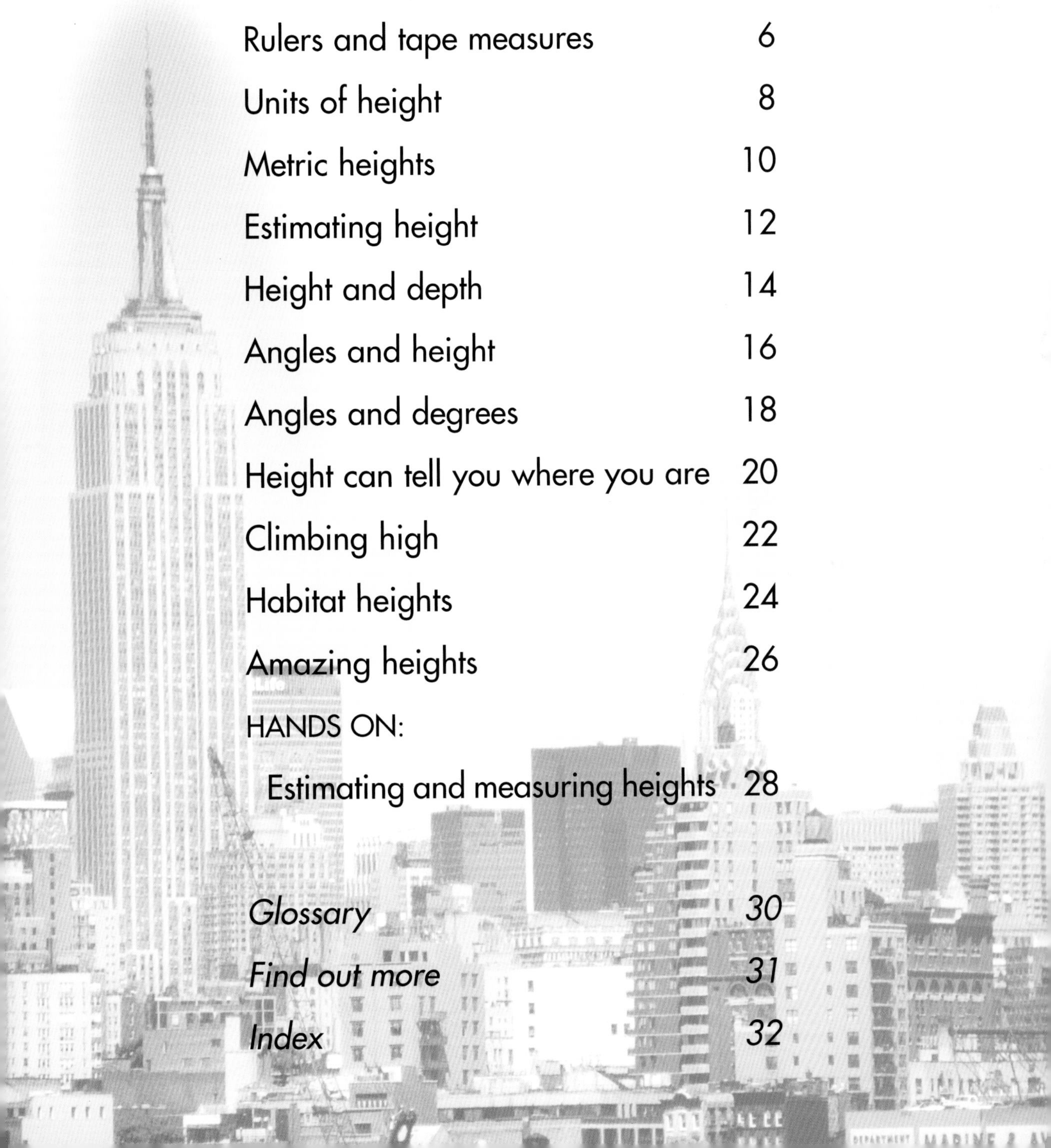

What is height?

Anyone who has ever been to a big city has seen the skyscrapers towering overhead. The Empire State Building in New York City, for example, is one of the most famous skyscrapers in the world. It is also one of the highest. It reaches 1,250 feet (381 meters) into the air. If a few hundred schoolchildren could stand on one another's shoulders, they would be about as high as that building!

Height is a measurement. It is just like distance. The height of the Empire State Building is how far it goes up in the air.

In your dreams

People are a tiny bit taller when they wake in the morning than when they go to bed at night. During the day, a person's weight squeezes the body downward. It squashes the bones in a person's back so they take up less room. When someone lies in bed, the bones stretch out again.

When you go to sleep, your body relaxes and even gets a tiny bit taller!

Length is a measurement along the ground. Measuring length is the same as measuring distance. Suppose we could lay the Empire State Building on its side. Then we could measure its height by measuring how long it stretched down the street. So measuring height is really the same as measuring length or distance.

The Empire State Building is 1,250 feet (381 meters) tall.

Rulers and tape measures

We can measure shorter distances with a ruler or a tape measure. We can measure height just the same as we measure length. But we have to use the ruler pointing upward instead of lying flat or sideways.

Different rulers and tape measures come in different lengths. A school ruler is usually about 1 foot, or 12 inches (30 centimeters), long.

This boy's height is around 4 feet 3 inches (130 centimeters).

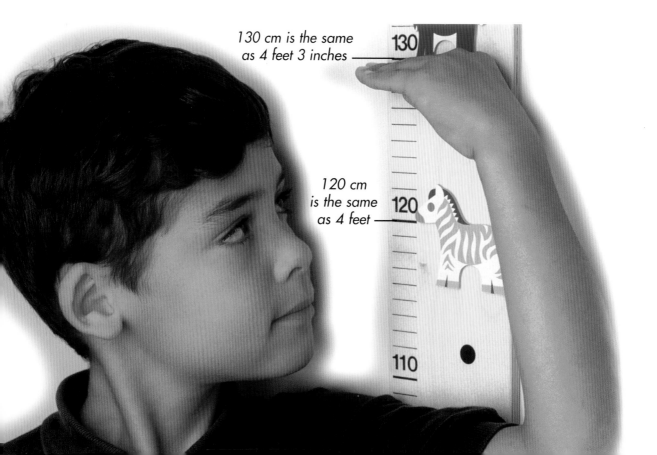

130 cm is the same as 4 feet 3 inches

120 cm is the same as 4 feet

How to measure your height

Stand against a wall and put a book flat on top of your head. Turn around but keep the book in place. Make a small pencil mark on the wall just under the book. Ask an adult's permission first! Now use a ruler or tape to measure the distance from the pencil mark to the ground. That measurement is your height.

A yardstick is 3 feet, or 36 inches (90 centimeters) long. For measuring longer distances, we have to use a tape measure. Tape measures can be any length from a few feet to hundreds of feet. Sometimes tape measures wrap onto a reel with a handle to make them easier to use.

Rulers and tape measures have lines marked along the side to show measurements. These lines are called the scale.

Make sure your heels touch the wall when you measure height like this.

Units of height

When we use a ruler or tape measure, we usually read height in yards, feet, or inches. We could use a ruler and find that a small bird is about 6 inches high. With a tape measure, we might find an adult is 6 feet tall. If we stood on a ladder, we could measure the height of a house. We might find it was 6 yards high.

Units are important
The house, the person, and the bird all measure six. But the house is taller than the person, who is much taller than the bird. The number six means something different each time.

The height of a house is measured in yards. To paint the outside of a house, we need to know the house's height and length. Then we can figure out the area of each wall (height x length = area) and how much paint to buy.

We call yards, feet, and inches the units of measurement. A unit is part of a measurement. It tells how big the measurement is. A yard is bigger than a foot, and a foot is bigger than an inch.

How high is that?

Different animals have very different heights. Here are the heights of some common ones:

Fly   ¼ inch
Earthworm   ¼ inch
Lizard   1 to 2 inches
Cat   1 foot
Dog   6 inches to 3 feet
Human   5 to 6 feet
Horse   5 to 7 feet
Giraffe   15 to 19 feet

A giraffe is hundreds of times larger than a fly or an earthworm. We measure small things in inches and larger things in feet.

Metric heights

Inches, feet, and yards are called imperial units. The imperial system of measurement is the commonly used system in the United States. In other parts of the world, people commonly measure heights with different units. These units include millimeters, centimeters, and meters. This other way of measuring is called the metric system.

Changing heights

If 4 feet are the same as 1.2 meters, 8 feet must be the same as 2.4 meters. We can always change feet and inches into meters and centimeters. The following table gives some height measurements in both imperial and metric units.

1 inch is the same as 2.54 centimeters

<u>1 inch (2.54 cm)</u>

1 foot, or 12 inches, is the same as
    30 centimeters
1 centimeter is the same as 0.4 inches,
    or ⅖ inch
1 meter, or 100 centimeters, is the same
    as 3 feet 3 inches

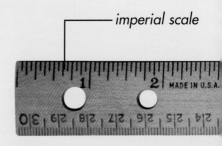

imperial scale

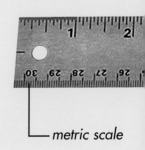

metric scale

One metric centimeter (cm) is smaller than half an inch. There are 2.5 cm in an inch. A hundred centimeters make 1 meter (m). And a hundred meters make 1 kilometer (km).

Metric rulers and tapes

Rulers and tape measures are usually marked with either imperial or metric units. Sometimes a ruler or tape has inches down one side and centimeters down the other. Sometimes a tape measure has inches on one side and centimeters on the other side. That means a person can use the same ruler or tape to measure in either imperial or metric units.

You could measure your height with a tape measure and find that you are 4 feet tall. But the same tape might also tell you

Rulers often show both the imperial and metric scales.

that your height is 1.2 meters. These measurements look different but they are not. Your height does not change just because you measure it in different ways. A height of 4 feet is exactly the same as 1.2 meters.

Estimating heights

When a person finds something's height with a ruler, that is called a measurement. A measurement is usually very careful and exact. But we do not always have to measure something to find its height. Sometimes we can figure it out just by looking. That measurement is called an estimate because it is not exact. If you know that you are about 4 feet (1.2 meters) tall, you can

If you know how tall one person in this line is, you can estimate the height of the others by comparing them to that person.

probably guess how tall your friends are. Some friends will be taller, and some will be shorter.

It is easiest to estimate the height of something if you have already measured something else first. Suppose you have measured the height of a cat. Now suppose a dog stands beside it. You can probably estimate the height of the dog quite easily. But if you had not measured the cat, it would be harder to figure out the height of the dog.

Good estimates

Say you estimate the height of a dog and then measure it. If your estimate was close to the measurement, that was a good estimate. If your estimate was a long way off, that was a bad estimate. An estimate is different from a guess. With an estimate, we want to be as accurate as possible. With a guess, accuracy does not really matter.

This dog is about twice the height of the cat.

Height and depth

Buildings and people have height because they stand up above the ground. There is also another kind of height that goes down, sometimes deep underground. That measurement is depth.

For example, water can be deep. A swimming pool may be 3 to 6 feet (1 to 3 meters) deep. The ocean is much deeper than this. The farther out someone goes from the shore, the deeper the water gets.

Measuring depth

People measure the depth of the ocean in different ways. Sometimes they lower measuring ropes over the side of a ship. These ropes have weights tied to them to make them sink. People can also use sound to measure the ocean depth. They send a beam of sound down from a ship. Then they time how long it takes for the

These men are lowering a device called a depth gauge into the ocean. When it reaches the bottom of the sea, it tells them how deep the water is.

sound to bounce back up off the ocean floor. That tells them how deep the water is.

Into the deep

The world's oceans are not the same depth all over. The deepest part of all the oceans is a place called the Mariana trench, which is off the northern coast of Australia. Ocean trenches are deep slits in the seafloor.

The Mariana trench is 7 miles (11 kilometers) deep. If that distance was laid in a straight line along the ground, it would take about two hours to walk from one end to the other!

Scientists explore ocean trenches in submersibles like this one.

Divers use special equipment called scuba-diving gear so that they can breathe underwater. With no scuba gear, a person can only dive down to 100 feet (305 m).

Angles and height

If you stand up straight against a wall, you are at your full height. But if you stand a little distance away from the wall and lean back to touch it, your body will not reach up the wall so far, and you will not reach so high. The more you lean, the less high up the wall you reach. Try it and see!

When one thing leans against another, it makes an angle.

An angle is the space between two lines that cross or meet. A small angle means there is not much space between the lines. The lines are almost parallel. Parallel lines run in the same direction and never meet. A big angle means there is a lot of space between the lines. The bigger the angle, the farther apart the two lines are.

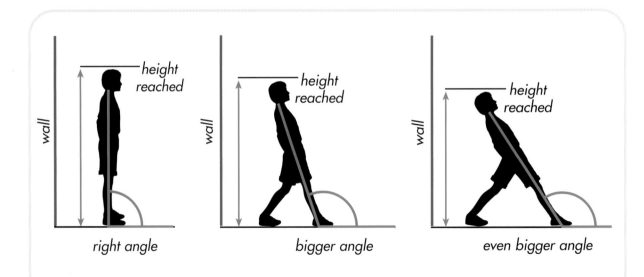

wall — height reached — right angle

wall — height reached — bigger angle

wall — height reached — even bigger angle

The more you lean against a wall, the less high up the wall you reach and the bigger the angle you make.

Right angles

A square corner is a special kind of angle. When two lines meet so that they make a boxlike corner, we call this a right angle.

A right angle is like one corner of a square. Many of the things around us are made with right angles.

Look carefully at these pictures. How many right angles, or corners, can you see in the chair, picture frame, and climbing bars?

17

Angles and degrees

The measurements we make with a ruler are usually in inches. So a ruler's scale is marked with inches. But we do not measure angles in inches. Instead, angles have their own units called degrees. And degrees are

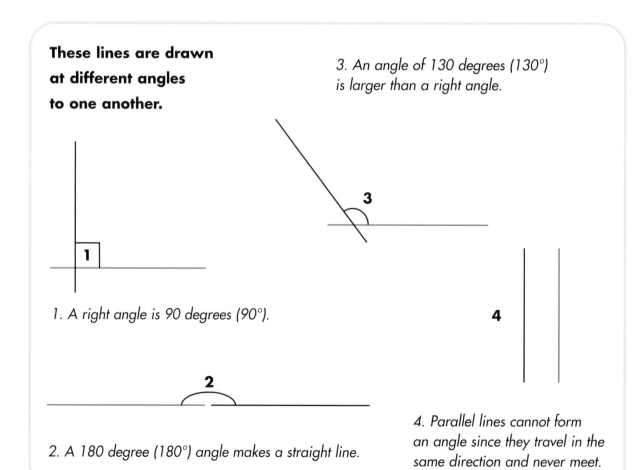

These lines are drawn at different angles to one another.

3. An angle of 130 degrees (130°) is larger than a right angle.

3

1

1. A right angle is 90 degrees (90°).

4

2

2. A 180 degree (180°) angle makes a straight line.

4. Parallel lines cannot form an angle since they travel in the same direction and never meet.

Using a protractor

A protractor has a target mark at the center of its bottom edge. To measure an angle, you put the target mark on the point where the two lines meet. You line up the protractor so one of the lines runs along the protractor's zero line. Then you see where the other line meets the scale. You measure the angle by reading it on the scale.

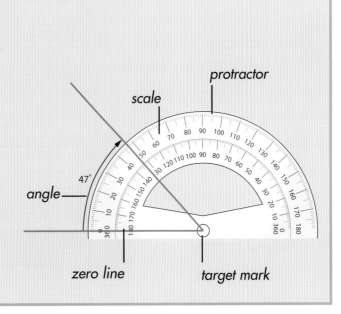

measured with a protractor. A protractor is like a curved ruler. Instead of measuring inches, it measures degrees.

Suppose we draw two lines that are parallel (the same distance apart). There is no angle between them. We say the angle between them is zero degrees or 0°. The symbol ° is just a quick way to write degrees.

To make an angle, two lines must cross or meet. We can draw lines at different angles to one another. The bigger the angle, the farther apart the lines are.

If we draw two lines at 90 degrees, they make a square corner or right angle. At an angle of 180 degrees, the two lines form a straight line.

Height can tell you where you are

Finding out where in the world you are is called navigation. Modern ships navigate in many different ways. Before modern methods were invented, it was much harder for sailors to know where they were. Sailors often found their way using the stars in the sky.

Sailors could measure their position using a sextant. This instrument was first used in the

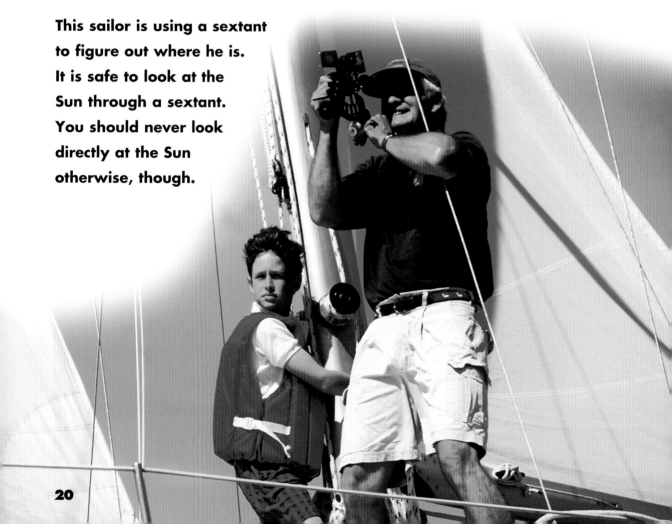

This sailor is using a sextant to figure out where he is. It is safe to look at the Sun through a sextant. You should never look directly at the Sun otherwise, though.

Quadrants

Before the sextant was invented, sailors used a device called a quadrant. Quadrants work on the same principles as sextants, but quadrants are simpler. Sailors used quadrants to measure the angle of the Sun, the Moon, or a star above the horizon.

The quadrant takes its name from its shape, which is a quarter of a circle. The curved edge of a quadrant is divided into 0 to 90 degrees. A small weight, or plumb-bob, of lead or brass is attached to the quadrant's right-angled corner. A sailor using the quadrant holds it so the plumb-line falls across the degree scale. Then the sailor looks along the straight edge until the star or Moon is in line with the sights. The angle is then read on the scale. Using this angle and the time of the day, the sailor can figure out how far north or south of the equator the boat is.

line of sight

sights

star

degree scale

plumb-line

plumb-bob

1730s. A sextant is like a small telescope fixed to a protractor. Sailors use sextants to measure the angle of the Sun, the Moon, or a star above the horizon. This is a type of height measurement.

With this angle, sailors can figure out how far north or south they are from the equator, as long as they also know the time of day. (The equator is the imaginary line that runs around the center of Earth.)

Although sextants were invented hundreds of years ago, sailors still use them today.

Climbing high

Gravity is the force that pulls things toward Earth. It gets weaker the farther away from Earth you go. One of the things gravity pulls toward Earth is air. Gravity squeezes the air and makes air pressure. That makes the atmosphere, which is the air we breathe.

Gravity is weaker at the top of a mountain than at

Altitude and altimeters

An airplane's height above Earth is called its altitude. Airplane pilots cannot measure their height easily—they cannot dangle a tape measure out of the plane until it reaches the ground! Airplanes measure their height with an instrument called an altimeter. It works by measuring the air pressure. Then it changes this measurement into the altitude.

An airplane's control panel always includes an altimeter.

the bottom. At the mountaintop, the weaker gravity means there is less air pressure. That makes it much harder to breathe than at the bottom of the mountain. The higher up you go, the lower the air pressure becomes.

There are many scientific instruments for measuring pressure. They are called barometers. If we measure air pressure with a barometer, we can use it to find out how high up we are. That can be very useful for measuring the height of a mountain.

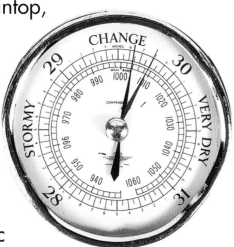

Barometers like this one are used to measure air pressure.

The higher up a mountain you climb, the lower the air pressure, and the harder it is to breathe.

Habitat heights

There are millions of different types of animals living on Earth. Each species, or type, of animal is best suited to living in a particular type of place. The type of place an animal lives in is called its habitat. A polar bear's habitat is the frozen Arctic. An alligator's habitat is a freshwater swamp or river.

Heights and depths

For many animals, height or depth is an important feature of their habitat. In a rain forest, for example, different types of animals live at different heights. Rainforest trees can be more than 200 feet (61 meters) high. A few giant trees grow even taller. Trees in a rain forest make layers, like the stories of a building. The top branches get lots of sun. The layers get darker farther down. Different animals live in each layer.

In the oceans, the same is true. The deeper the water, the darker it gets. And different animals are best suited to each layer.

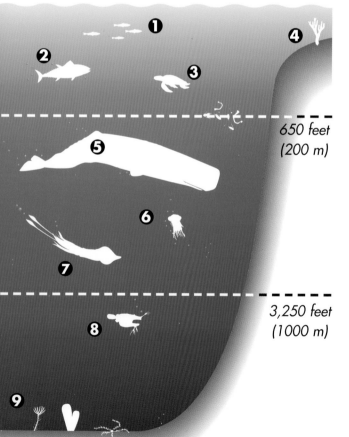

650 feet
(200 m)

3,250 feet
(1000 m)

Herring (1), tuna (2), sea turtles (3), and corals (4) live in the sunny top layer of the ocean. Sperm whales (5) and jellyfish (6) live in deeper, darker waters but visit the surface to feed. Giant squid (7) and deep-sea angler fish (8) stay in the dark depths. Sponges and brittle stars (9) live on the seafloor.

Rainforest layers

Canopy
The treetops form a crowded, leafy roof called the canopy. Many birds and climbing animals live in the canopy.

Understory
The understory is shaded from the sun by the canopy. Butterflies, snakes, and anteaters called tamanduas live in the understory.

Forest floor
Little light reaches the forest floor. Jaguars, warthogs, peccaries, and other animals live down here.

harpy eagles

toucan

spider monkey

sloth

emerald tree snake

blue morphos

tamandua

jaguar

warthog

peccary

Amazing heights

We can find out some amazing things by measuring heights. If no one ever measured heights, we would never know the height of the world's tallest man. He was named Robert Pershing Wadlow and he lived from 1918 to 1940.

This Great Dane towers over a tiny terrier dog.

The world's tallest man, Robert Pershing Wadlow, with his normal-sized brothers.

When he was last measured, he had grown to the height of 8 feet 11 inches (2 meters and 72 centimeters)!

Other animals can also reach amazing heights. One of the world's tallest breeds of dog is called the Great Dane.

A Great Dane usually grows to a height of nearly 3 feet (90 centimeters). That is taller than a lot of young children.

Horses can also be very tall. Many horses grow to heights of 6 to 7 feet (1.8 to 2.1 meters).

Tallest buildings

Listed here are some of the tallest buildings in the world. Each one is the same height as hundreds of 6-foot (1.8-meter) adults standing on one another's shoulders.

Tall building	How high is it?	How many people tall?
KVLY-TV mast, North Dakota, USA	2,063 feet (628 meters)	344 people
CN Tower, Toronto, Canada	1,815 feet (553 meters)	303 people
Taipei 101 skyscraper, Taiwan	1,667 feet (508 meters)	278 people

The CN Tower in Toronto, Canada, is 1,815 feet high.

Estimating and measuring heights

1 Get one friend to stand straight against a wall. Mark where the top of his or her head is on the wall with the chalk. Be careful not to damage the wall. Ask someone's permission first. Or, instead of marking the wall, hold a small ruler on the wall where the top of your friend's head reaches.

2 You or your friend can measure down from the mark or ruler to the ground. Write down the height on paper.

Always write down the units!

When you measure height, the measurement you make has two parts. One part is the number you read off the ruler or tape measure. The other part is the units, such as inches or centimeters, that the ruler or tape measures. If you just write down the number 6, no one will know if that means 6 inches, 6 feet, 6 centimeters, or 6 meters. So always write down the units and not just the number.

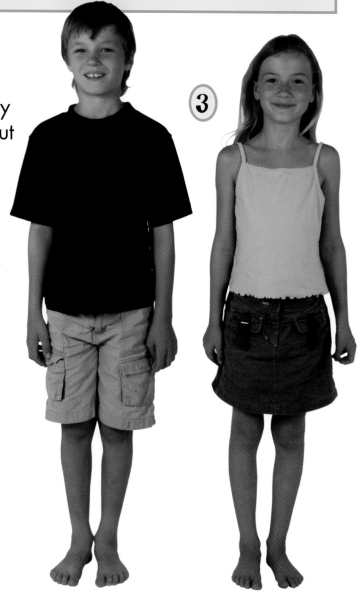

3 Now move on to your other friends or family members. Look carefully at each person and think about their heights. Are they taller or shorter than the person you just measured? How much taller or shorter? Estimate each person's height. Write down what you think the height of each person is.

3

4 Now measure their heights just as you did for the first person.

5 Were your estimates close? You should find that you get better and better at estimating as you go along.

Glossary

altimeter A device in an airplane that measures height.

altitude Height above sea level.

angle The space between two lines that cross or meet.

atmosphere The gases (air) we breathe that surround Earth.

centimeter A small distance equal to one meter divided by 100.

degree A unit for measuring angles.

depth Height that goes downward.

distance A measurement of the space between two points.

foot An imperial distance equal to 12 inches (or 30 centimeters).

height A distance between two points, measured upward.

imperial The commonly used system of measurements in the United States. The imperial system is based on inches, feet, and yards.

inch An imperial distance, which is the same as 2.5 centimeters in the metric system.

gravity A force that pulls things toward Earth.

length A distance measured sideways or along the ground.

meter A metric measurement equal to 3 feet 4 inches.

metric A set of measurements based on the meter.

navigation A way of finding a position on Earth, at sea, or in space.

parallel A pair of lines that never meet or touch.

protractor A device for measuring angles.

right angle A 90 degree angle.

ruler A straight measuring tool.

satellite An uncrewed spacecraft that can measure things from space.

scale The marks on the side of a ruler, tape, or protractor.

sextant An old-fashioned device used for navigating at sea.

tape measure A long, flexible ruler.

yard An imperial distance equal to 3 feet, which is the same as 90 centimeters in the metric system.

Find out more

Books

Carol Vorderman, **How Math Works.** New York: Penguin, 1996.

Frances Thompson, **Hands-On Math: Ready-To-Use Games and Activities For Grades 4–8.** New York: John Wiley, 2002.

Greg Tang and Harry Briggs, **Math for All Seasons.** New York: Scholastic, 2002.

Jerry Pallotta and Rob Bolster, **Hershey's Milk Chocolate Weights and Measures.** New York: Cartwheel Books/Scholastic, 2003.

Web sites

Empire State Building
Web site of one about one of the world's highest buildings
www.esbnyc.com

FunBrain.com Kids Center
Maths and measurement games
www.funbrain.com/measure/ index.html

Robert Pershing Wadlow
The tallest person ever
www.altonweb.com/history/ wadlow/index.html

Science Made Simple
Metric conversions for length measurements
www.sciencemadesimple.net/ EASYlength.html

Index

airplane	22
air pressure	22, 23
altitude	22
altimeter	22
angles	16–17, 18–19, 21
Arctic	24
atmosphere	22
barometer	23
canopy	25
centimeters	10, 11
CN Tower, Toronto	27
degrees	18, 21
depth	14
depth gauge	14
distance	4
divers	15
Earth	22, 24
Empire State Building	4, 5
equator	21
estimates	12, 13, 28–29
feet	9, 10
forest floor	25
gravity	22, 23
Great Dane	26, 27
habitats	24
horizon	21
imperial units	5, 10, 11
inches	9, 10, 18, 19
KVLY-TV mast, North Dakota	27
length	5, 6
Mariana Trench	15
measurements	18, 21, 28–29
meters	10, 11
metric system	10, 11
millimeters	10
Moon	21
mountain	22, 23
navigation	20, 21
ocean	14, 15
parallel lines	18, 19
plumb-bob	21
protractor	19
quadrant	21
rain forest	24, 25
right angles	17, 18, 19, 21
rulers	6, 7, 8, 11, 18
scale	7, 11, 19, 21
scuba diving	15
sextant	20, 21
sound beam	14
stars	20, 21
submersible	15
Sun	20, 21
swamp	24
tape measures	6, 7, 8, 11
understory	25
units	8–9, 18, 29
Wadlow, Robert Pershing	26
yards	8, 9, 10
yardstick	7